MW00365700

WELCOME!

Welcome to your Get Courageous Journal. As a coach, I've learned that information isn't powerful unless you're given a chance to act on it. I believe journaling is the most powerful action you can take to get the maximum benefit from *Get Courageous Now* and I am thrilled to share this exclusive journal with you.

The Get Courageous Journal is going to take you on the journey of a lifetime. You will discover more about who you are, begin to take action on what you've learned, and make solid plans for the future. The journal is broken into the same Chapters as *Get Courageous Now*. It includes all of the Courageous Action Steps plus 4 other categories of reflection questions. Please note that at times the Courageous Action Steps have been modified and placed in different sections of the journal, but they are all still there along with many other resources for your personal growth.

Get Courageous Journal

The Get Courageous Journal is meant to be a companion to *Get Courageous Now* and includes more in-depth exercises and a special place for reflection. The first 12 chapters include 5 types of questions to encourage you to interact with the text, action steps, and yourself. These are:

Courageous Connection: This is the first section you will come to as you are journaling. The Courageous Connection seeks to help you connect yourself to the material by thinking about who you are now and where you've come from.

Courageous Self-Assessment: The second section of each chapter will give you an opportunity to assess how you are performing in each of the areas we cover. This may include rating yourself or reflecting on different events in your life.

Define to Conquer: Here at the Get Courageous Movement™, we believe that defining is the first step to succeeding. You need to have your own definition of the terms and concepts that we discuss so that you can better interact with the information. Here you will define courage, fear, purpose, and even— yourself.

Courageous Action Steps: In each section, the Courageous Action Steps are where we encourage you to do something in your life to act on what you've learned. At times, these action steps are the same as the book, but occasionally we have moved the action steps to other categories and focused on giving you varied tasks so that you can begin to apply what you've learned right away.

Courageous Lessons Learned: We close each section with Courageous Lessons Learned. In *Get Courageous Now*, I give you a brief summary of each chapter. But, in the Get Courageous Journal, you are going to write down and reflect on the lessons you've learned. This is always a free-write to allow you to reflect, summarize, and remember the steps that you've committed to take or have taken throughout the chapter.

7 Day Courageous Challenge

Chapter 13 has a different format than the rest of the chapters. The 7 Day Courageous Challenge from *Get Courageous Now* has been reprinted in its entirety in the journal for your convenience. We have given you space to reflect, and added an additional Take It Further section that is exclusive to the Get Courageous Journal. We trust that this last section will help you to begin your life of courage right away.

Extra Journaling Pages

In addition to each action-packed companion chapter, we have included numbered blank journal pages in the back half of the book. We specifically wanted to number these so that if at any time you run out of room to express yourself in the given chapter, you can continue writing in the back and note the page number in the chapter itself. We want to give you the freedom to explore all that you need to— and we want you to be able to clearly look back at your journey.

I hope that his journal will become a trusted ally to discovering your purpose and passions and living them out courageously. Throughout this journal, I encourage you to reach out to me as your resource and let me know about your triumphs. You can always tweet me **@KikiRamsey** and tell about your **#CourageousJourney**. Throughout the journal, we have included additional challenges and I would love it if you'd take the time to let me know that you've completed them. I want to be your coach and your mentor. As this method begins to change your life, let me know. That's personal encouragement to me, letting me know that I'm living out my passions and purpose as I help you find yours.

Well, with that, I think it's time for you to launch your journey! Grab *Get Courageous Now*, a pen, and a bit of peace and quiet (if you can manage it) and start reading and responding to Chapter 1.

CHAPTER 1: THE COURAGE WITHIN YOU

Welcome to the first Chapter of your new Get Courageous Journal! In this chapter, I'll be introducing you to the courage that is already within you. We'll discuss your courage, your fear and its connection to your childhood, and the Courageous Promise that you are going to make to yourself. So go ahead, find a quiet place to read, think, reflect, and write as you take this first step in your courageous journey.

Courageous Connection

1. When did fear first show up in your life?

____

____

____

____

____

____

____

2. Were you courageous as a child? Write about a time when you showed courage when you were young.

____

____

____

____

____

3. Name a time that fear made you feel trapped. What happened as a result of your fear?

____

____

____

____

____

____

Courageous Self-Assessment

Rate yourself on a scale of 1 to 10 with 10 being the most courageous:

____

Why did you decide on that number?

____

____

____

____

Define to Conquer

What does courage mean to you? Write a personal definition of courage.

Write a personal definition of courage.

____

____

____

____

____

Courageous Action Steps

Your Courageous Promise

Write a promise to yourself about your new, bold, and courageous outlook on life. Promise yourself to conquer fear, to be successful, whatever you think is most important. Make it personal, and refer to it often. This is the vision statement for your courageous journey. Need an example? See mine on pg. 22.

My Courageous Promise:

"Everybody has the potential for courage. You don't have to be born with courage; you can learn to be courageous."

What are 3 areas of your life where you can begin to exercise your courageous muscle? List the area of life with a specific action step. For example, “I can exercise courage at work by submitting my ideas about increasing sales to my boss.”

1.____

2.____

3.____

Courageous Lessons Learned

It's time to recap. What are your takeaways from Chapter 1? What did you learn about the courage within you?

CHAPTER 2: YOU WERE MADE FOR A PURPOSE

Now that you've made a Courageous Promise to yourself, it's time to discover your purpose and your passion. Throughout this Journal section, you'll be answering purpose-driven and passion-driven questions, defining PURPOSE in your life, assessing where you are now, and taking our #BucketListChallenge. Are you ready to go on a journey of discovering your passion and purpose? Let's get started!

Courageous Connection

We all have a purpose. Do you know what yours is? These 8 Purpose-Driven Questions will help you narrow down what you were made to do.

1. What are you great at?

____

____

____

____

____

2. What are your strengths?

3. What hurts you? What makes you cry, makes you angry, or gets under your skin?

4. What things do you value most? Why?

5. Who do you admire? What qualities do you like most about that person?

6. What would you do for a living if you didn't have to worry about money?

____

____

7. Name a cause you are willing to fight for.

____

____

8. What services can you provide to better individual lives and the world as a whole?

____

____

"If God Himself has given you a purpose in life, surely you can be courageous enough to proclaim it with joy and confidence."

Our Purpose is driven by our Passion. Your passion and your purpose lead you to your life's work. Now that you've narrowed down your purpose, let's see how much it lines up with your passions.

Here are 7 Passion-Driven Questions. What are your passions?

1. What new things do you want to try?

____

____

2. When you were younger, what did you want to be when you grew up?

____

____

3. What activities do you like now?

____

____

4. What makes you smile?

____

____

5. What makes you get excited?

____

____

6. What things do you secretly like, but haven't told anyone about?

____

____

7. What places do you want to travel to?

____

____

Courageous Self-Assessment

At this point in your life, how well do you believe you are living out your passion and purpose? Are they a part of your daily life? If not, are you working towards goals that will help you to better live out your passions and purposes everyday?

"For I know the plans I have for you, plans to prosper you and not to harm you. Plans to give you a future and a hope."
-Jeremiah 29:11

Define to Conquer

I have shared my personal acronym for P.U.R.P.O.S.E on pages 24-26, so what is your personal definition? You can make your own acronym, or just write it out.

Passion is the right hand of purpose. What does passion mean to you?

Courageous Action Steps

The Bucket List Challenge

Are you ready for this? Let's take discovering your passions and purposes to a whole new level. I want you to think about all the things you want to do before your time on earth ends.
Write **100** for me. Really. You can do it, just keep writing!

1. ______________________________
2. ______________________________
3. ______________________________
4. ______________________________
5. ______________________________
6. ______________________________
7. ______________________________
8. ______________________________
9. ______________________________
10. ______________________________
11. ______________________________
12. ______________________________
13. ______________________________
14. ______________________________
15. ______________________________
16. ______________________________

17. ______
18. ______
19. ______
20. ______
21. ______
22. ______
23. ______
24. ______
25. ______
26. ______
27. ______
28. ______
29. ______
30. ______
31. ______
32. ______
33. ______
34. ______
35. ______
36. ______
37. ______
38. ______
39. ______
40. ______
41. ______
42. ______
43. ______
44. ______

45. ____
46. ____
47. ____
48. ____
49. ____
50. ____
51. ____
52. ____
53. ____
54. ____
55. ____
56. ____
57. ____
58. ____
59. ____
60. ____
61. ____
62. ____
63. ____
64. ____
65. ____
66. ____
67. ____
68. ____
69. ____
70. ____
71. ____
72. ____

73. ______________________________
74. ______________________________
75. ______________________________
76. ______________________________
77. ______________________________
78. ______________________________
79. ______________________________
80. ______________________________
81. ______________________________
82. ______________________________
83. ______________________________
84. ______________________________
85. ______________________________
86. ______________________________
87. ______________________________
88. ______________________________
89. ______________________________
90. ______________________________
91. ______________________________
92. ______________________________
93. ______________________________
94. ______________________________
95. ______________________________
96. ______________________________
97. ______________________________
98. ______________________________
99. ______________________________
100. ______________________________

Let's narrow that list down a bit. You have 100! Great job! Now, I want you to go through and choose your top 10. Just 10. Write them below.

1. ____________________
2. ____________________
3. ____________________
4. ____________________
5. ____________________
6. ____________________
7. ____________________
8. ____________________
9. ____________________
10. ____________________

Great job! Now, let's cut that list in half. Are you ready for this? Let's narrow it down to your Top 5.

1. ____________________
2. ____________________
3. ____________________
4. ____________________
5. ____________________

Awesome! Now it's time for the final challenge. Your Big 3. What are 3 things you want to do the most before you die?

1. ______________________________

2. ______________________________

3. ______________________________

Reflect:

What do these 3 things show you about your passions and purpose? Do they line up with your answers in the Courageous Connection section?

____

____

____

____

____

____

____

You've finished the challenge and I want to hear all about it! Tweet me **@KikiRamsey** with **#BucketListChallenge** and tell me what you've learned, that you've completed the challenge, or your Big 3.

Purpose, Passion, Action! Name 3 things you can do to move towards a life full of passion and purpose this week. Be specific.

1. ______________________________

   ____

2. ______________________________

   ____

3. ______________________________

   ____

Courageous Lessons Learned

If you've stuck with us this chapter, chances are you have learned A LOT about who you are and what you want out of life. You can't grow until you know! Let's take a second to recap. What are your takeaways from these exercises?

CHAPTER 3: WHAT IS YOUR FEAR FACTOR?

Get ready Courageous Journaler— in Chapter 3, we're going to come face to face with your fear. We are going to discuss how fear interacts with your life and calculate your Fear Factor. At the end of this chapter, you will know how much fear is costing you every day, week, month, and year. You will also see how fear is keeping you from spending your time the way you want to. Grab a pencil or pen and your copy of Get Courageous Now and let's dig in.

Courageous Connection

Fear isn't all bad— it's goal is to keep us safe. Let's spend time reflecting on fear— the good and the bad

> "Fear is always going to do the job it was commissioned to do. It is your job to tell fear that it needs to go away."

1. When is a time fear was a positive emotion in your life? When did fear actually help you by keeping you safe?

___

___

___

___

___

___

___

2. When is a time fear was a negative emotion in your life? When did fear actually hinder you from doing what you wanted to do?

___

___

___

___

___

___

Courageous Self-Assessment

Calculate your **#FearFactor** (pgs. 32-35)

Many of us have goals. Some we're too afraid to write down. Often times, fear keeps us from these goals.

The two biggest resources we have are time and money. How far off are you from your goals in this area? Could it be purely based on your fear?

Your Monetary Fear Factor

Step 1: Write down how much money you would like to make a month in box A below. It doesn't matter what you are making now, if you are a stay at home mom or an executive. Think about your gifts and abilities and the things you value in life and dream big.

Step 2: Write down how much money you are currently making each month. Be sure to include all income sources from your business, job, or side jobs. Write this in box B.

Step 3. Subtract Box B from Box A. Write the total below. This is your Fear Factor.

A. ______________________

B. ______________________

Fear Factor: ____________________

Take a minute and look at that number. Do you think this is what fear is costing you on a monthly basis? Think about it for a second.

Now, let's break that down even further.

What is your fear costing you per week?

Fear Factor: ___________ ÷ 4 = ___________

Let's really bring this home.
What is your fear costing you every day?

Fear Factor: ___________ ÷ 30=___________

Last Step: What is fear costing you in annual income?

Calculate it below.

Fear Factor: ___________X 12 = ___________

Take a minute to look at these numbers. Do you think this is an accurate representation of what fear is costing you? What are you thinking? What are you feeling? Write it here.

"For every challenge that you face, you must do the work to overcome it."

Your Fear Factor and Your Time

Do you value time more than or equally to money? Calculations aside, let's just look at your time. Do you have the freedom and the ability to spend your time how you'd like to and how you were meant to? Answer these questions to begin your journey.

How many people in your life do you wish you had meaningful, positive relationships with?

How many people do you actually have these relationships with?

How many new things did you want to try in the last year?

How many did you actually try?

How many interesting opportunities presented themselves to you within the last year?

How many did you actively pursue?

Now, let's look at this on a weekly level. What are 5 things that you'd really like to do during the week? How many hours would you like to devote to them? How many are you devoting to them? Fill in the chart below.

Activity	Hours you'd Like to Spend	Actual Hours
1.		
2.		
3.		
4.		
5.		

Define to Conquer

This entire chapter is focused on identifying fear in your life and what it could be costing you on a daily, weekly, monthly, and yearly basis. But, before we continue to talk about this concept, let's create your own definition of fear. By putting this abstract concept into your own words, you will have a better knowledge of what we are going to seek to conquer in the rest of this book.

What does fear mean to you?

Courageous Action Steps

You've determined your Fear Factor in both time and money. Now, let's make an action plan.

What are three actions you can take this month to begin narrowing the gap of your monetary fear factor?

1. ____________________

2. ____________________

3. ____________________

What are three actions you can take this week to begin using your time the way that you'd like to?

1. ____________________

2. ____________________

3. ____________________

Is there anything that you need to cut out of your schedule to meet your time goals? What about your monetary goals? List these things here.

Courageous Lessons Learned

You did it! You have analyzed your life and figured out the gap between where you are and where you want to be! I'm so proud of you! Now it's time to start fighting. But before we say goodbye to this chapter and forge ahead, write down what you've learned so that it will stay with you. And remember, if you enjoyed finding your **#FearFactor**, tweet me **@KikiRamsey**. I'd love to hear about your personal journey!

What have you learned this chapter?

CHAPTER 4: THE EIGHT MAIN FEARS THAT HOLD PEOPLE BACK

In Chapter 3, we introduced you to fear— its positives, negatives, and what it's costing YOU. Now, we are going to give that Fear a Name so you know how to fight back with courage. Let's figure out your top three fears, how they are uniquely yours, and come up with some ideas to start fighting back.

Courageous Connection

In this chapter, I've laid out 8 major fears that could be holding you back (pgs. 37-49). How do these eight fears affect you? List them in order of your biggest fear to your smallest below.

1. ______________________________
2. ______________________________
3. ______________________________
4. ______________________________

5. ______________________________

6. ______________________________

7. ______________________________

8. ______________________________

What do you think your top and bottom fears tell you about what is most important to you in life?

____

____

____

____

____

____

____

____

Courageous Self Assessment

Now that you've listed your top 8 fears, let's take a closer look at your top 3.

List them here:

1. ______________________________

2. ______________________________

3. ______________________________

Reflect on these three fears by writing about a time in your life where one of these fears made you feel trapped or negatively influenced your decisions. Write about each fear.

Response 1

____

____

____

____

____

____

"Put your fear aside and take the padlock off so you can discover your destiny."

Response 2

Response 3

Define and Conquer

Let's look at your **#Top3Fears** again. I described all of these fears for you in the chapter, but you are unique. How would you describe your top 3 fears? The more you know about them, the more you will be able to conquer them.

Definition of Fear 1:

____

____

____

____

____

____

Definition of Fear 2:

____

____

____

____

____

____

Definition of Fear 3:

____

____

____

____

____

Courageous Action Steps

Name 3 actions you can take this week to begin facing one of your fears. Be specific.

1. ____

   ____

2. ____

   ____

3. ____

   ____

Courageous Lessons Learned

What have you learned about yourself and your unique fears throughout this chapter?

"You have the ability to be and do anything you want in this lifetime, but only if you believe it and are willing to do what it takes to make it happen."

CHAPTER 5: STEP 1- YOUR AWAKENING

You've completed Part 1 of *Get Courageous Now* and are ready to move on to Part 2— The 7 Step Courageous Process. This step-by-step process will be transformational in your quest for a courageous life. In Step 1, we're going to be talking about Your Awakening. It's time to take a good look at yourself, define your reality, and get rid of past baggage by forgiving those who have harmed you. Are you ready for a power-packed journaling session?

Courageous Connection

When was a time in your life where you had an awakening to reality? What happened? How did you feel? What was the result?

____

____

____

____

____

____

What is something that has happened to you that you need to accept responsibility for and let go?

____

____

____

____

____

____

Courageous Self Assessment

What negative emotions are present in your life the most? Is there anything about that you would like to change?

____

____

____

____

____

____

Think through the things that are upsetting to you about the past. How many people do you simply need to forgive?

"The key to handling the realization that your life may not be all that you want it to be is to acknowledge exactly where you are in life."

Define and Conquer

Forgiveness is a heavy word and an essential action to a positive, happy, and healthy life. What does it mean to you? Is this definition helping or harming your ability to forgive?

Define your reality. What is the current reality of your life? By acknowledging the present, you will begin the process of setting yourself free.

Courageous Action Steps

For today's first Courageous Action Step, we are going to get serious about forgiving. Think about what you wrote down in your Forgiveness Self-Assessment. How many people do you need to forgive?

You are going to write 2 forgiveness letters (see examples on pgs 66-67). One to yourself, and one to someone else. Make these personal. They are for you to express your feelings, forgive, and finally let go.

Dear ________________,

Dear ________________,

Think about a negative emotion or situation you've recently had or been in. Now, think of how you could have used the 4 steps to Managing your Emotions, found on pages 63-65, in that scenario. How would it have helped? Would the situation have had a different outcome?

"You were meant to live an amazingly good, happy and healthy life and its time you embrace this fact."

Courageous Lessons Learned

Wow! Step 1 of the Courageous Process is no joke! We covered your awakening, acknowledged your reality, discussed forgiveness, and learned about managing your emotions. So, what are your Courageous Lessons? Write them below to help them stay with you throughout your courageous life.

CHAPTER 6: STEP 2- MAKE A DECISION

You've looked in the mirror and come face to face with who is really looking back at you. Maybe that was tough. Maybe there were things that were hard to see. But wasn't it— freeing? You saw yourself— and that's the best starting point there is. Now, we are going to make a decision that will power us through the rest of this process. We're going to be looking deep at those lifelong dreams and latent desires and we're going to give them life— and wings. Let's get going! I'm so proud of you for taking this journey and I believe in you!

Courageous Connection

What do you truly want out of life?

If money were not a factor, what career would you pursue? What would your life look like right now?

____

____

____

What are some things that you have been dying to do?

____

____

____

What are your current dreams?

____

____

____

"In order to get what you want, you have to know where you are going."

Courageous Self Assessment

Where are you with your promise in Chapter 1? How can you renew this commitment to yourself?

Define and Conquer

How is a decision different than a choice? What makes a decision stick?

What kind of a decision maker do you think you are? What is your decision making process like?

____

____

____

____

____

____

____

____

____

Courageous Action Steps

If you're not ready to make decisions, you're allowing life to push you along wherever it will take you. It's time to face these decisions and take control of the things that are in your power. In this action step, you will define a direction, a destination, and some checkpoints along the way. You will also begin to seriously consider what you are willing to give to your dream.

Step 1: What is your direction? What do you want your life's purpose to be? Where are you going?

____

____

____

____

Step 2: What is your destination? Where is the next place you want to end up? Is this 5 years from now? 20 years from now? A lifetime?

____

____

____

____

____

____

____

____

____

Step 3: Map out some checkpoints. Break your destination, your big dream, or goal, into separate steps with a time frame. For example, if your goal is to have a certain amount for retirement in 20 years, break that down into what you should have in place every 5 years.

Think through the destination and break it into your own weekly, monthly, yearly, or 5, 10, 20 year checkpoints.

Step 4: What are you willing to give? I mentioned on pages 72-73 that we have to be willing to give to our goals. Now, let's make that concrete.

How much money are you willing to give each month to achieving your destination?

How much time are you willing to give each week to this goal?

"You are beautiful. You are fabulous and wonderfully made. You deserve all the goodness life has to provide, so why not go after what is rightfully yours?"

Courageous Lessons Learned

From your awakening to making a decision, you are 2 Steps into my transformational 7 Step Courageous Process. What have you learned about making decisions? Did this bring clarity to your goals? Did it help to define how much you need and are willing to give to these dreams? Write about it here!

CHAPTER 7: STEP 3- DISCOVER WHO YOU REALLY ARE

Who are you? It's a question that many of us wrestle with our whole lives. We try to find our identity in our career, wealth, spouse, kids— but we need to realize that who we are when all of that is taken away is still valuable and infinitely important. Today, you're going to face your past and remember. We're going to discuss your transparency level and look at how your past affects your present. But most importantly, we're going to challenge you to define yourself. And that's a journey worth taking. Let's get ready to discover who you really are.

Courageous Connection -- Remembering

In today's Courageous Connection, I want you to face your past. I want you to focus on remembering, no matter how distant or difficult it is. Let's look in the past and just take a chance to remember.

What is your very first memory?

What was your overall childhood experience?

What were your teen years like?

What were you told about your future when you were growing up?

What circumstances or experiences have affected your adult life in a major way?

"Discovering and accepting your true self and being vulnerable enough to show the world who you really are takes real courage."

Courageous Self Assessment

How transparent are you? How often do you let people see the real you? Do you often hide behind clothes or makeup? Do you pretend you have it all together? Do you hold back your true opinions and beliefs in unhealthy ways?

____

____

____

____

____

On a scale of 1 to 10, how transparent and real are you with your family?

What about your friends?

Strangers?

What do the above questions show you about yourself?

____

____

____

____

____

____

____

Define and Conquer

Throughout your journal, I've been asking you to define almost every key term we discuss. Why? Well, I believe defining increases understanding and allows us to connect with the material and the change we need to bring into our lives. Today, we're going to define something entirely different. Actually, this is going to be the most important definition you ever write. It is time to define— yourself.

Who are you? Who are you really? Write a Who I Am Statement to define who you are. Dig deep and accept yourself for who you are— because you are uniquely and wonderfully you.

Need an example? See mine on page 101.

"Finding out who you are is the biggest puzzle you will ever solve. Once you discover the real you, you'll wonder where you've been hiding all these years."

Courageous Action Steps

So far in this Chapter's Journal, you have remembered your story, assessed your transparency, and defined who you are. Now, let's connect these together by analyzing your story. We are going to discover how your past still affects your present. As we work through this, I want you to come up with one action step you are going to take to begin working through any negative connections. Maybe you need to make an appointment with a therapist or life coach. Maybe you need to acknowledge something, or forgive, or make a decision for change. That's up to you. But let's think through how our past affects our present and how we can create a brighter future.

What childhood circumstances or situations affect your life today?

____

____

____

____

Action Step

____

____

What problems are you experiencing today that were also present in your past?

____

____

____

____

Action Step

____

____

Do you have a positive, optimistic outlook on life or a generally negative, pessimistic outlook? How does this current attitude relate to the attitude you had growing up? How does this attitude affect your life right now?

Action Step

What do you believe about money? Is that at all connected to what you were taught as a child?

Action Step

What do you believe about health and fitness? What were you taught growing up?

____

____

____

____

Action Step

____

____

What do you believe about going after your dreams? Does this have a connection to your past?

____

____

____

____

Action Step

____

____

What were your religious beliefs? Did you grow up having a spiritual practice or believe in a deity or deities? Is this your faith today?

Action Step

Do you have great romantic and non-romantic relationships in your life? What did your past teach you to believe about relationships?

Action Step

Did you have a lot of drama in your household growing up? Does this affect your house now?

Action Step

Was your family emotionally attached or emotionally removed? What about you?

Action Step

What things were you told about life that you have been holding onto until today? Do you need to let any of them go?

Action Step

What is your overall attitude about life right now and why is it like this? What were your parent's general attitudes about life?

Action Step

What are your true values? What things do you care about the most? What things did you care about the most growing up?

____

____

____

____

Action Step

____

____

How does your life differ now than when you grew up? Is this a positive or negative difference?

____

____

____

____

Action Step

____

____

If you could change anything about your life what would it be and why?

____

____

____

____

Action Step

____

____

What is one action step you can take in order to enact the change you want to see in your life?

____

____

____

____

Action Step

____

____

Courageous Lessons Learned

Great job! You have just completed a major feat—remembering and analyzing your story as well as defining Who You ARE! Congratulations! With this many in-depth questions, I'm sure you learned something about yourself. Record it here for future reference and to see how far you've come!

CHAPTER 8: STEP 4- IDENTIFY THE REAL PROBLEM

Now that we've delved into a bit of history and you are one step closer to knowing yourself, we need to look at some of your problems. Everyone's got them. There's no need to shy away. In this section, you're going to identify surface problems in your life and try to discover the root issue. Then, we're going to see how these fit into the 6 Main Areas of Life and make an action step to work on them. It's time to face the issues so that we can reap the rewards of growth.

Courageous Connection

Let's look at the areas of your life and try to define the root problems. In the first column, quickly list out your problems. Don't think about surface or root, just list the problems that come to your mind.

THEN analyze each one and try to figure out what the root problem is.

For more information on Surface vs. Root, see pages 103-105.

Surface	Root

Now, sort each of your problems into one of these six areas. This will show you which area you need to do the most work on in your life and which areas you are excelling in.

Emotional	Physical	Spiritual

Relational	Financial	Career

Courageous Self Assessment

We've identified some key issues in your life and have sought to see what the root problems are. Now, I want you to do a more general assessment. On a scale of 1-10, how satisfied are you with where you are in the 6 areas below? Why?

Emotional: ____

____

Physical: ____

____

Spiritual: ____

____

Relational: ____

____

Financial: ____

____

Career: ____

____

Define and Conquer

What is your definition of a problem? How does this affect how you go about your daily life?

____

____

____

____

____

____

Courageous Action Steps

You have now rated yourself on the 6 biggest areas of your life and have seen how many problems are dwelling in each of these areas.

Now, it's time to take action. Looking at a list like this can be daunting, but you can simplify it by focusing on just 1 action step for each area of your life that you can begin to work on. This should be something that you can easily act on in the next week or month.

Emotional Action Step:

____

____

Physical Action Step:

____

____

Spiritual Action Step:

____

____

Relational Action Step:

____

____

Financial Action Step:

____

____

Career Action Step:

____

____

"Surface problems are issues that manifest themselves based on a root problem that goes to the heart of the issue."

Courageous Lessons Learned

In Step 4, we've identified problems and made an easy to implement action plan. What are you going to take away from these discoveries that will help you to be a more courageous you this week?

"The key to identifying the real problems in your life is identifying that true root issue and dealing with it accordingly."

CHAPTER 9: STEP 5- DEVELOP A NEW AWARENESS

Step 5 of the 7 Step Courageous Process invites you to a new level of awareness. We are going to focus on positivity and combating our negative self-talk as well as working towards discovering your vision for your life. Finally, you're going to get the opportunity to hit the ground running on your dreams by going on a Vision Stretching Mission, all while cultivating an attitude of gratitude.

Courageous Connection

Do you believe that anything is possible? Why or why not? How can you build your belief?

Do you believe you are powerful? In what areas of your life are you most powerful? In what areas are you more powerful than you think you are?

How open are you to hearing the truth about yourself and your life? Is there a trusted friend who can see into your life? Could you help yourself grow by asking them what areas of weakness they see in you?

"Power is a mighty force inside of all of us waiting to be used to our advantage. Power is our ability to control or influence others or ourselves."

If you were wealthy and had all of the needed resources at your disposal, how would you start your day? Where would you wake up at? What would your activities be?

____

____

____

____

____

Now, what would the rest of your day look like? Would you be working? What would that job be like? What would you do in the evenings?

____

____

____

____

____

"Power is a mighty force inside of all of us waiting to be used to our advantage. Power is our ability to control or influence others or ourselves."

Courageous Self Assessment

On pages 111-113, I talked about a high and low level of awareness. If we are highly aware, we are in tune with every detail of our surroundings and have an incredible focus. Low awareness is like functioning on auto-pilot.

What areas of your life are you highly aware of? What areas of life do you have a lower awareness?

____

____

____

____

____

How many low awareness areas need to become areas of high awareness for you to be successful?

____

____

____

____

____

Positivity vs. Negativity

Are you generally a more positive or negative person?

____

____

____

____

Visualization

How good are you at visualizing your goals? Do you do it often? How would you like to improve in this area?

____

____

____

____

Define and Conquer

At times it is easy to be positive with others or with external events, but when it comes to ourselves, we are negative. In this section, I want you to define 5 areas of your life where you tend to be negative towards yourself or your situation in life and list them here.

1. ______________________________

2. ______________________________

3. ______________________________

4. ______________________________

5. ______________________________

Now, let's redefine these negatives. I want you to write 5 power-packed positive statements to combat against those negative emotions. Repeat these to yourself every time that negative thought or emotion surfaces.

1. ______________________________

2. ______________________________

3. ______________________________

4. ______________________________

5. ______________________________

Courageous Action Steps

Vision Stretching Mission

I want you to go on your very own vision stretching mission like I described on pages 118-120 and on page 125. By this point in *Get Courageous Now*, you should know what your dream, direction, and destination are. Think creatively and find a way to visit a dream career, dream job, or anything else in line with your vision to show you what one day might be a reality in your life.

Write a detailed reflection of the event here. What thoughts and feelings did you have? Also, I love hearing about what you discover, so tweet me **@KikiRamsey** with **#VisionStretchingMission** and tell me all about it!

Attitude of Gratitude

It is easier to be positive when we assume an attitude of gratitude. One way to do this is to keep a gratitude journal to keep a record of all the things you are thankful for. You can make your own, but to get you started, I'm going to challenge you to do a **#Thankful50.**

What are 50 things, in any order, that you are thankful for?

1. __________
2. __________
3. __________
4. __________
5. __________
6. __________
7. __________
8. __________
9. __________
10. __________
11. __________
12. __________
13. __________
14. __________
15. __________
16. __________
17. __________
18. __________
19. __________
20. __________
21. __________
22. __________
23. __________
24. __________
25. __________
26. __________
27. __________

28. ______________________________
29. ______________________________
30. ______________________________
31. ______________________________
32. ______________________________
33. ______________________________
34. ______________________________
35. ______________________________
36. ______________________________
37. ______________________________
38. ______________________________
39. ______________________________
40. ______________________________
41. ______________________________
42. ______________________________
43. ______________________________
44. ______________________________
45. ______________________________
46. ______________________________
47. ______________________________
48. ______________________________
49. ______________________________
50. ______________________________

If you finish this list, give me a shout out **@KikiRamsey** with **#Thankful50Challenge**. And hey, maybe share 3 of your favorite things to be thankful for to inspire others to live with an attitude of gratitude.

Courageous Lessons Learned

We've had another power-packed journaling session with Step 5 of the Courageous Process. I hope that you are discovering who you are and how to live your purpose. Make a record of all that you learned here so that in moments of doubt you can see how far you've come!

CHAPTER 10: STEP 6 - CREATE A PLAN

Step 6 involves looking back. We're going to be flipping back to chapter after chapter of this journal and looking at your responses. We're going to pull together your passion, purpose, decisions, and dreams and make a plan for courageous success in those areas. And this time, we're going to follow through.

Courageous Connection

It's time to recap. As we begin to plan, we need to look back over all of the self-discoveries you've made throughout this book. So let's get started!

Flip back to Chapter 2 and remind yourself of your answers to your purpose and passion driven questions.

Now, look again at your bucket list. Are you still happy with your BIG 3, or do you see a different level of importance now?

Look at your Who Am I statement in Chapter 7 and remind yourself what you are here for.

Lastly, look at your Direction and Destination in Chapter 6 and see if that is still what you believe.

Reflecting on your journey will help you as we begin to make plans.

Courageous Self Assessment

As we get ready to plan, here are some questions that can help you assess where you are and where you want to go.

What are my real problems? What did I discover in Step Four?

What do I want to change about my life and my situation?

What are my career goals?

What goals do I have for my family? Where would I like to see them in 5 years?

What are my financial goals? What are my plans for saving, budgeting, and retirement?

____

____

____

____

What are my spiritual goals? How do I plan to enhance my relationship with God and/or with the world I am a part of?

____

____

____

What are my physical or health goals? How do I plan to maintain or obtain a healthy weight? How do I plan to eat better?

____

____

____

Define and Conquer

What is your personal definition of a plan?

Is planning a positive or negative experience for you? Why?

Courageous Action Steps

Look at the Assessment questions and consider what you discovered in your Courageous Connection. Now, I want you to make 3 plans. These need to be attainable plans. They can be anything you want them to be, but be sure you follow the correct format as seen on page 131 and below.

Here is the format:

1. State the Problem

2. State the Goal
   Use the SMART Method, found on pages 129-130.
   Specific
   Measurable
   Attainable
   Relevant
   Timely

3. Answer the Why Question.
   Why am I doing this?

Now it's your turn. Write out 3 plans on the blank pages that follow. We have left these pages unlined so that you can scribble, brainstorm, and draw out a plan in a way that suits you.:

> All plans are not created equal. The strength of a plan depends on how much work, time, and research you are willing to put into it."

Plan 1

Plan 2

Plan 3

"Creating a plan with some great goals is the best way to overcome your problems and create a better future for your life."

Courageous Lessons Learned

What did you learn about planning and goal setting this chapter? How are you going to use it to better your life in the future?

CHAPTER 11: STEP 7- TAKE ACTION

You're almost finished with the 7 Step Courageous Process! Look at how far you've come! Your hand may be sore from writing and you may have shed a few tears on the journey, but it is one of growth and healing. Now that you've made your 3 Plans in Step 6, we are going to show you how to take action by identifying your **#FirstSteps**. Let's get started on building a life you love and want today.

Courageous Connection

When is a time in your life that you decided to Take Action on a plan that you had made? When did you decide to do something to better yourself or your family? How did that go? How did it make you feel? Do you mostly have positive emotions associated with taking action?

____

____

____

____

____

"Creating a plan with some great goals is the best way to overcome your problems and create a better future for your life."

Courageous Self Assessment

Have you made plans before? If so, how dedicated are you to following through with them? Do you enjoy the process and then stop there? Or do you continue until you've reached the goal?

____

____

____

____

____

Name one plan in your life that you have succeeded in and one you have not taken action on. What was the difference?

____

____

____

____

____

____

Define and Conquer

What does taking action mean to you? What mental image comes into your head? What do you think this image says about you?

____

____

____

____

____

Courageous Action Step

Flip back to Chapter 10 and look at your 3 plans. Now, I want you to make a Next Action Step for each plan. This should be a simple first step that can get you on the right track to following through on your plans.

Plan 1, Step 1:

____

____

Plan 2, Step 1

____

____

____

Plan 3, Step 1

____

____

____

Now, pick 2 plans that you are most ready to start.

Take Step 1 on those two plans this week.

Then tweet **@KikiRamsey** about your **#FirstActionStep** in the **#CourageousMovement.**

Courageous Lessons Learned

This chapter is all about ACTION! What did you learn about the way you took action in the past? How are you going to overcome that this week as you take your First Action Steps for two of your plans?

"Don't be discouraged by the challenges that come your way. Great people are born by overcoming great challenges and doing great things."

CHAPTER 12: NO MORE EXCUSES

Congratulations! You've completed the 7 Step Courageous Process and are on the right track to success, but we have to be wary of the things that will try to get in your way. Now, we are going to get face to face with your excuses and your blame. We need to take back the power in our lives and make choices, not excuses. Let's reflect and learn how to avoid excuses so that our plans will succeed.

Courageous Connection

Every single one of us gives into excuses at some point or another. In this section, we are going to look at 30 different excuses. 29 are the most common, and 1 should be uniquely yours. Check the box next to all of the excuses you are making.

> "Fear shows up as excuses, which are just bad reasons to let ourselves off the hook from doing things that really scare us but are important to our overall success."

Courageous Self Assessment

- ☐ I don't have enough time.
- ☐ I am just not good enough to do what I want to do.
- ☐ I don't know how to do what I'm trying to do.
- ☐ I don't know enough to do what I want to do.
- ☐ I don't know what I want.
- ☐ I don't know my purpose.
- ☐ I'm too tired by the end of the day to work on other stuff.
- ☐ There are not enough hours in the day for me to get it all done.
- ☐ It's just too hard.
- ☐ I'm always too tired.
- ☐ My full-time job is holding me back.

- □ The children require too much time.
- □ I'm too old to go back to school.
- □ I will never be successful because success is for other people.
- □ I will never make it because I don't have enough money.
- □ No one wants to buy what I have because I just got started.
- □ I am not motivated to complete the tasks I need to do.
- □ I don't have enough money to do everything I need to do for my business.
- □ I don't have enough help to do everything I need to do.
- □ I have to work so I can make money because my own business is not making money; therefore, I don't have time to devote to my own business.

- ☐ I don't want to fail so I need to do more research.
- ☐ I'm not creative so I need to look at what everyone else is doing.
- ☐ I can't teach or talk about money because I'm not good enough.
- ☐ No one supports my dreams
.
- ☐ Other people are judging me, so I won't try.
- ☐ I can't go to that meeting because someone will judge the car I'm driving.
- ☐ I just don't have time to exercise.
- ☐ I can't go to that seminar even though it might change my life because I need a babysitter, I need to sleep, I don't have the money, or I need to drive around aimlessly thinking of something to do.
- ☐ Your own personal excuse:

____

____

____

As we get started in this chapter's journey, think about these questions and assess where you are with excuses, blame, and self-limiting behavior.

1. How many excuses did you check above?

2. How much power in your life have you given away to excuses instead of deciding to make choices?

3. Do you consider yourself to be a blamer? How often do you blame others for the circumstances you are in?

4. How often do you find yourself listening to your self-limiter?

Define and Conquer

What does blaming mean to you? Write a definition and a description of blame. If blame were a person or a creature, what do you think it would look like?

Courageous Action Steps

Look at your journal for Chapters 6 and 7. Write one of your most important goals below. Then, in the excuses area, list every excuse you've ever given yourself about achieving that goal.

GOAL

Excuses

Now, for every excuse you listed above, I want you to write one reason why you can achieve your goal. List these here.

Circle your top 3 reasons and write them here:

Top 3 Reasons to Succeed

1. ____

____

2. ____

____

3. ____

____

Congratulations! You now know your Top 3 Reasons to Succeed! You can use these to combat your self-limiter and your excuses.

Every time you doubt, remind yourself— you can succeed and you have reasons to back you up.

"Be brave, open up your mouth, and tell the word your passions and dreams."

Courageous Lessons Learned

So, in this chapter, we've discussed your excuses, your blame, your power, and your choices. What did you learn about this? What are you going to take away to help you courageously move towards your goals?

CHAPTER 13: THE SEVEN DAY COURAGEOUS CHALLENGE

Congratulations! If you have really dug into the work and into yourself these past 12 chapters, you are ready for the courageous journey of a lifetime. Before we release you to your passion-infused, purpose-driven courageous goals and plans, we'd like to give you one last challenge. The 7 Day Courageous Challenge.

This challenge was designed with YOU in mind. It's time to take our new-found knowledge from our heads to our daily lives. Over the next 7 days, you will be taking action steps for your future.

I know you can do this and I want to be your courageous coach. I'll be with you every single step of the way, so feel free to give me a shout out **@KikiRamsey** about your **#7DayCourageousChallenge**

Follow along with each day's objectives and write a reflection here in your journal.

Want an additional challenge? Exclusive to the *Get Courageous Journal* are Take it Further sections, which provide you with bonus ideas to build on what you learn each day.

Day One: Face Yourself

To know who you are is one of the greatest gifts you can give yourself and those you love. Begin this journey by taking some time to think and answer these questions:

What do you want out of life? Forget what you've always been told you should want and consider the truth of what would actually make you happy.

Why aren't you living the truth that you wrote about above?

What are you afraid of? Mentally, emotionally, financially, socially? What things produce fear in your heart?

What are your personality flaws? Do you give up easily? Will you bully or manipulate to get what you want? Do you struggle to be honest with loved ones? Do you allow your self-limiter to get in the way of your success?

Reflect

When thinking about and answering these questions today, what did you discover? What did you feel? What can you do to act on the knowledge you received today?

"Everyone was placed on earth with at least one gift. It is your job to use your gift(s) for the benefit of others as often as you can."

Take it Further

Find a close friend or family member that you can trust. Consider sharing with them what you've learned about yourself today. Share your goals and dreams with them and ask if they will help support you while you chase them. Write about what happened as a result!

Day 2: Do Something That Scares You

As babies, we are fearless. We take that first step, say that first word, and pick up unfamiliar things with little regard for consequence. We have infinite courage that, over time, is either reinforced or stripped away by life events.

Today, recapture some of that fearlessness by doing something that scares you. This can include things like:

-Starting a conversation with a stranger
-Asking someone out or telling someone you love them
-Asking for a promotion
-Being truly vulnerable, open, honest, and transparent with someone you love
-Volunteering to speak in public
-Leaving a comfortable situation for the unknown

Choose something that frightens you or that you would otherwise avoid, but not something that could put you at risk or cause harm to you or another.

Reflect

What did you choose to do? Why? Reflect on what you did and how it made you feel. Did it make you feel stronger or more fearful?

Take it Further

What other fears do you need to face with action? Are you ready to commit to a new Fear-Facing challenge? If so, I want you to try to do something you fear every day for 30 days. Write down each activity here and explain how it helped you on your journey.

1. ______________________________
2. ______________________________
3. ______________________________
4. ______________________________
5. ______________________________
6. ______________________________
7. ______________________________
8. ______________________________
9. ______________________________
10. ______________________________
11. ______________________________
12. ______________________________
13. ______________________________

14. ____________________

15. ____________________

16. ____________________

17. ____________________

18. ____________________

19. ____________________

20. ____________________

21. ____________________

22. ____________________

23. ____________________

24. ____________________

25. ____________________

26. ____________________

27. ____________________

28. ____________________

29. ____

30. ____

Day 3: Do Something New

We don't grow or learn from doing the same things all of the time. So today, do or try something you've never experienced before. This can be something simple, or something complex, but no matter what, it is significant.

> "Where there is passion, there is purpose, and where there is purpose, there is a lifetime of happiness."

Reflect

What did you choose to do today? Why? Was it hard for you to decide what you wanted to do? Why or why not? Did you enjoy what you did? How did it make you feel?

Take it Further

What other new things would you like to try? Make a list of at least 10, but don't let that number stop you! Write down as many as you can think of.

Day 4: Do Something for Someone Else

There is courage in forging you own path, but there is also courage in being willing to sacrifice on behalf of others. Use today to give a bit of your time for someone else. What are you going to do to serve someone you know? Or someone you don't know?

Reflect

What did you choose to do and why? Was it difficult to decide on something to do? How did it make you feel to help someone else? What did you have to sacrifice to do it?

"We all have two voices inside of us, one that cheers us on and one that tries to knock us down."

Take it Further

Consider making service a part of you and your family's weekly or monthly lives. Research charities, non-profits, and organizations in your community and see if you could donate time each week or one Saturday a month to serving others. If you make a new commitment, I would love to hear about it. Tweet me **@KikiRamsey** and tell me about how your **#CourageServes**.

Day 5: Create Something

It takes courage to put your time and energy into creating something. As children, we overflow with creative energy and ingenuity. Over time, we become discouraged from that part of ourselves.

So today, I'm challenging you to take some time to create something. Whether that's drawing a picture, writing a poem or story, sewing, knitting, arranging flowers, a DIY home improvement project, whatever you like!

Don't agonize over it. Just do it. Put your focus into letting your mind drift and flow as it will. Don't judge, don't edit, and don't second guess. Create.

Reflect

What did you choose to create today? Why? What did it feel like to free yourself to create? Was it harder or easier than you expected? Would you show this to a friend? A stranger? Why or why not?

Take it Further

Some of you may have just created something for the first time in a while. Others of you may be naturally creative. Maybe this challenged helped you to get back to something that you love. If that's the case, I am encouraging you to find a way to make this a part of your life again. Find a new creative hobby, or see if there is a potential business for you with this challenge. Any new ideas? Tweet me **@KikiRamsey** and tell me how **#CourageCreates** in your life.

Day 6: Commit to Ending Something

Just as we can get into ruts and fail to try new things, it's also easy for us to cling to behaviors, habits, and thoughts that are no longer serving us well. Today, you are challenged to put an end to that. Today is the day you commit to and act on ending something. What are you working to end?

Reflect

What did you choose to end today? Why? Have you ever tried to end this before? How long did it last? What is going to make this time different? How can you be successful?

Take it Further

Let's think more deeply about this behavior. What scares you about it? How is it ingrained in your personal narrative? What in your past influenced the start of this habit? More importantly, what keeps it going?

"Courage is your right. It is yours to embrace and use regardless of how you look, what you have, or where you live."

Day 7: Commit to Beginning Something

Yesterday, I challenged you to end something that was no longer serving you. The great thing about endings is that they leave the door open for new beginnings.

Today, start something new and positive for yourself. What are you going to start? What action are you going to take to begin today?

Reflect

What did you choose to begin? Why? What action did you take? How can you make your new thing a part of your daily, weekly, and monthly life?

Take it Further

Write a plan for incorporating your new beginning into your life. Are you trying to save money? Decide on a goal and a plan for what to save each month. Are you starting a business? Make a plan. Are you starting a diet? Ditto. You need a plan. Review the SMART Goals and Plan-making strategies we've covered in Chapter 6, and write a plan here.

Congratulations!

You've finished 12 chapters of life-changing material and our **#7DayCourageousChallenge**. I'm so proud of you!

Any final thoughts as you reflect one last time on your week?

WELCOME TO YOUR NEW, COURAGEOUS LIFE!

You did it.

If you have made it to the end of this book and journal, if you have dug in and given it all you have, then you are a different person today than you were when you started.

You've really sat down and figured out what you want. You've discovered your purpose, your passions— and your fears. You've found out who you are, and who you want to be.

And now, I challenge you to live your unique, courageous journey.

But just know, I will be with you every step of the way in whatever way you'd like me to. Whether that is through my website, where you can sign up for weekly Newsletters and Courageous videos, my Get Courageous Seminar, or personally, as your courageous life coach, I desire to be a part of your journey.

Because your journey to courage is a part of mine— as you allow me to speak into your life, I am able to fulfill my purpose, my passion, and exercise courage.

I hope to hear from you soon, and I can't wait to see the courageous woman I know that you will become.

With all the best of luck, blessings, and good wishes upon you,

I give you this final charge:

Live courageously, fearlessly, and purposefully -- and find your passionate life of fulfillment.

Until next time,

~Kiki Ramsey

CPSIA information can be obtained
at www.ICGtesting.com
Printed in the USA
BVHW040830270219
540690BV00013B/8/P

9 780692 766149